Dumb Men and the Women Who Love Them

A collection of true stories about that "guy thing" and its effect on love and marriage and the uselessness of maps while driving in strange cities

Peter Taylor

Fitzhenry & Whiteside

Dumb Men and the Women Who Love Them
Copyright © 2002 Fitzhenry & Whiteside

Fitzhenry and Whiteside Limited
195 Allstate Parkway
Markham, Ontario L3R 4T8

In the United States:
121 Harvard Avenue, Suite 2
Allston, Massachusetts 02134

www.fitzhenry.ca godwit@fitzhenry.ca

Fitzhenry & Whiteside acknowledges with thanks the Canada Council
for the Arts, the Government of Canada through its Book Publishing
Industry Development Program, and the Ontario Arts Council
for their support of our publishing program.

10   9   8   7   6   5   4   3   2   1

National Library of Canada Cataloguing in Publication

Taylor, Peter
Dumb men and the women who love them / Peter Taylor.

ISBN 1-55041-742-8

1. Man-woman relationships—Humor. I. Title.

PN6231.M45T39 2002   C818'.5402   C2002-902685-7

United States Publisher Cataloging-in-Publication

Taylor, Peter.
Dumb men and the women who love them / Peter Taylor. —1st ed.
[136] p. : ill. ;   cm.
Summary: Based on daily newscasts and newspapers from around the
world, a collection of true stories about men who, caught between a rock
and a good woman, seem genetically programmed to head for the rocks.

ISBN 1-55041-742-8 (pbk.)

1. Men — Psychology.   2. Man-women relationships.   I. Title.
305.3/ 8 21   CIP   BF692.5.T39 2002

Design and typesetting: Kinetics Design
Cover image: courtesy Hulton Archives /Getty Images
Printed and bound in Canada

Introduction

THE stories you are about to read are true. All of them have appeared in newspapers from around the world or made their way onto radio and television newscasts. All of them — as some people insist on suggesting — involve that "guy thing;" that "je ne sais quoi" or genetic quirk which occasionally prompts grown men to think, not with the left or right — but with the backsides of their brains.

Curiously, or perhaps naturally, very few of the stories gathered for this book involve women attempting the manly arts of drinking and thinking while dealing with other important complicated stuff. Where women are involved, the reader will notice, they are frequently on the sidelines, innocent bystanders, or absent when the bizarre "guy thing" behavior kicks in.

It makes a body wonder, doesn't it?

If — as we are frequently reminded — there is indeed a great and wonderful woman behind every great and wonderful man, do the stories in this book suggest the kind of things that happen when she isn't there?

Is man pre-programmed from the moment of birth to drive the rest of the world insane with antics embarrassing even to the average orangutan?

Is the boy yanking on the little girl's pigtails truly the father of the man?

Can we fit "the guy thing" into the worlds of love, and marriage, and the world around us, or, as the following trail of stupidity suggests, is "the guy thing" too inbred in the genes and goofiness and trousers of man?

Should the following scientific report, in fact, be taken seriously?

The Guy Thing

SCIENTIFIC studies on several continents indicate that while baby girls do learn to walk at roughly the same age as baby boys, they fall significantly behind their male counterparts when it comes to eating worms, sticking foreign objects up their noses, squirting mashed potatoes through their teeth, riding tricycles down stairwells, and setting fire to neighbors' garages.

It is their mastery of these disparate talents, say behavioral specialists, that marks the dawning of the remarkable and ever-growing gulf between male and female children, boys and girls, obnoxious teenagers of both sexes and, ultimately, men and women.

In fact, it is the male child's ability to amuse, baffle, infuriate, spook, and yes, even scare the living bejeezus out of ordinary and innocent people that sets boys apart from all other creatures in the animal kingdom.

It is, say the authors of a groundbreaking work in child development, the birth of a behavioral pattern sometimes referred to as "socially unacceptable creativity," or, what is more commonly known as, "the guy thing."

While no reasons have been attached to the general absence of these diverse anthropological talents in little girls, the study says that such bursts of development in young males would appear to be both learned behavior on the one hand, while at the same time equally driven by some form of genetic coding on the other.

In a paper entitled "Random Observations at Suburban Intersections," Edward Cowan, a member of the Canadian study group and a specialist in unacceptable deportment, reported that in randomly chosen neighborhoods, boy children and girl children behaved in dramatically different ways when the driver brought the family automobile to a halt at a stop sign or traffic light.

"It did not seem to matter if the car was being driven

by the mother or the father. The minute the driver braked, the little girl in her little car seat looked out the window at the surrounding landscape, while the little boy in his little car seat rammed his little index finger up his little nostril."

"In short," Cowan summarizes, "young boys seem to pick their noses, scratch themselves in public, and belch simply because they can. With or without the influence of a male role model, these actions, talents, whatever you choose to call them, come naturally.

"What the boy child is saying, in effect, is, 'I can pick my nose, make farting sounds with my armpits, and eat Oreos until I get sick. Therefore I am.'"

Not surprisingly, another study found examples of equally inventive behavior at every stage of the male child's life from infancy through dotage.

What was surprising, the study's author suggests, is that the inventive behavior learned and mastered at each stage in what he calls "The Ages of Man" becomes a permanent part of manhood itself, and does not fall away or disappear with aging.

Thus, argues the author, at formal dinner parties or black-tie occasions of any sort, when one member of the group breaks wind, the jollity and humor of the incident is enjoyed equally by every man in the room from age 3 to age 63.

"What's funny is funny," explains American social scientist Jasper Reid, "yet we have been remiss in developing a working vocabulary to explain it."

Reid, author of the best selling *Grow Up: Why?* also prepared an extensive catalogue of normal behaviors for the various age groups. He points out that the commonality of experience and the unbounded glee males take in the embarrassment of others often results in the unfounded charge — by some — that men frequently behave like free-range children or unruly teenagers throughout their entire life spans.

In his chapter on male development, Reid suggests that by age 3 a normal male child will have already mastered such diverting and varied talents as mock tantrums in grocery stores, incontinence, spewing milk through his nostrils, squirting soft foods and liquids through the tiny gaps between his teeth, and driving the family pet to distraction.

By age 3, the young fellow may also have gathered several swear words as attention-getting devices, or what Reid classifies as "battle cries."

At age 4, a boy will have learned to belch on cue, search for belly-button lint in public, and will have learned to spoil mealtimes by stuffing himself with junk snacks and candy before lunch and dinner.

By now he should also be able to wet the floor, the walls, and the toilet seat while peeing.

By age 4, whenever the lad walks into the house, the family pet will know from experience to hide or skulk off to another room.

From ages 5 through 7, the little fellow should begin to teach much of the above behavior to younger siblings, though the author does suggest that while a little brother will remember these lessons for a lifetime, a younger sister will have forgotten them well before the year is out.

From 5 through 7, a normal lad will also begin to supplement his growing vocabulary with a healthy lacing of such words as brassiere, panties, boobies, boogers, cooties, penis, and pecker.

He should also have struck the fear of God into every available babysitter within an 8 block radius, and performed complicated medical procedures on visiting female cousins and playmates of the opposite sex.

By ages 8, 9, and 10, a healthy little scamp should have mastered the complicated technique of "mooning" and begun to invent the sorts of antics that drive school-teachers into early retirement. He may also have started to ape the way his father walks and sits, and will memorize for future use the way Dad sucks back brewskies straight from the bottle.

At 11 and 12, Reid further suggests, a normal guy learns to leave the toilet seat in the upright position (unless he's peeing), begins to leave heaps of soggy towels on the bathroom floor, and has begun to accumulate an arsenal of practices guaranteed to disturb, upset, or "gross out" his female classmates and neighbors.

By age 13, it is normal for a young man to have discovered his father's hidden stash of girlie magazines, to change his underwear or socks only when threatened by loss of kitchen (*read* refrigerator) privileges, and to possess his own TV remote.

As teenagers, normal boys begin to become the men they will be, and tag each other with endearing nicknames such as *dickweed, pizza-face, peckerhead, bozo, scumbag* and *stinky.*

Close to half "The Ages of Man" section deals with the teenage years 13 to 18, noting that it is during this particularly formative time when the influence of the opposite sex begins to play an important role in his development.

To attract the attentions of members of the opposite sex they employ peacockery, and shout crude greetings at each other when meeting on the street. Expressions such as "silent but deadly", "she's a nympho" and "huba-huba" join the lexicon of snappy phrases used to impress each other and the people around them.

By age 18, a normal youngster will have learned to wheel past his ex-girlfriend and her new beau at 140 miles per hour (in his father's car), and just knows when he walks away from an empty toilet paper roller that it will somehow be looked after by the time he returns.

It is this arsenal, this bag of tricks, this repertoire of values and talents that guides a young man into his 19th year, and genuine adulthood.

Armed to the teeth with everything he's learned from childhood to the present day, and knowing absolutely everything there is to know, the young man sets off in search of fame and fortune.

He understands the uselessness of maps and the dangers inherent in asking total strangers for directions while driving in strange cities and foreign countries.

Somewhere, he knows, there's a special someone who shares his dreams and desires, and above all else his finely honed sense of humor.

And yes, he knows, there's a lady out there who understands that while her instincts are inclined to cuddling after love making, her guy is equally compelled, through conditioning, and by every protein in his body, to seek out the refrigerator and stand before it, naked, motionless, silhouetted against its ghostly light.

It is this "guy thing" that makes a man a man — the million lessons learned from infancy to adulthood.

And it is this very "guy thing" — the gigabytes of memory required to retain all that he's learned and will ever know, that occasionally leads a man to do really *dumb* stuff.

For examples of the "guy thing" at large in the world around you, read on.

Dumb Men
and the Women
Who Love Them

I SHOULD HAVE MARRIED THAT GUY WHO PUKED ON ME AT MY HIGH SCHOOL PROM

CARDIFF

A SOUTH WALES woman has threatened to divorce her husband, saying she's "sick and tired of 'Charlie Boy'," the ventriloquist dummy her husband insists on bringing along when they sit down to watch TV, when they go to the supermarket, and even when they head out for a romantic evening.

The 41-year-old woman says she thought it was funny at first, but now she's totally fed up.

"He spends more time talking to a lump of wood than he does to me. If I had my way it'd be kindling. I can't even watch TV without the thing chipping in with smart-ass comments. He even sets a place for it at the dinner table."

Barry Roberts, 40, says he rediscovered his childhood toy in his mum's attic. He now spends several hours a day practicing his ventriloquism technique in front of a mirror.

He says he's sorry that Charlie Boy upsets his wife, but adds that every man needs a hobby to stop marriage from becoming dull.

Sure it's funny now — but what if someone had poked an eye out

PARIS

ADDING a dash of performance art to his bid for freedom, a 52-year-old French convict used superglue to cover himself with broken glass and sharp objects in the belief that prison guards would be unable and unwilling to grab him as he strolled out of jail.

With sharp wooden splinters, broken bottles, and razor blades covering his hands and body, the man headed for the prison gates.

Guards said he even had scissors glued to both his shoes.

Alas, his escape plans were foiled when a half-dozen guards, using blankets and cot mattresses wrestled him to the ground.

There are many women who'd have left him there to marinate . . .

PITTSBURGH

COURT officials called it the practical joke that backfired when a 44-year-old man, attempting to frighten his wife by pretending to be the victim of a burglary, smeared himself with tomato sauce, sprawled himself on the kitchen floor, and then fired a shot from a .22-caliber rifle straight up into the ceiling.

Police say the man's wife called emergency services after she heard the shot and found him laying prostrate on the floor.

Police refuse to say whether or not the man's wife was amused or frightened, but a federal judge found nothing funny in the dumb stunt, and sentenced the man — who had previous firearms offences — to 15 years in prison.

Now I ask you, why didn't I think of this when I was 21?

BERLIN

A 72-YEAR-OLD German nightclub owner had lawyers alter his will so that his entire estate — valued at close to $500,000.00 — would go to the last woman who slept with him before he died.

Rolf Eden, owner of one of the city's most famous discos, said he could think of no better way to go than in the arms of a beautiful young woman — "preferably under 30."

"I've put everything in my last will and testament," he explained to reporters. "The last woman who sleeps with me gets everything."

The sex-starved septuagenarian added that anyone considering his offer shouldn't put it off too long.

"I could go very soon," he said. "Possibly tomorrow."

Sacré bleu! My car keys, my glasses, and my watch appear to be stuck to zee buckle of your bra

PARIS

I N a story coming out of France, it appears that French men and French women are as poles apart as the rest of us.

Weary of living in the shadow of the "world's greatest lovers," American, Canadian and Englishmen the world over were pleased to discover that the Frenchman's claim to that title amounts to little more than a hill of haricots.

"One part wishes, nine parts *merde de taureau*," suggested at least one British tabloid.

Turns out that the average Frenchman is so klutzy and fumble-fingered when it comes to helping a woman off with her bra, that a lingerie manufacturer had to be called to the rescue before the story became a national embarrassment.

Velcro? Guess again!

Deciding that even Velcro would tax the buttery-fingered French, Bolero, a manufacturer working in concert with a behavioral consultant, opted for magnets.

Frustrated French are now hoping the new magnet bra will lead to more positive sexual relations, or negative . . . or something like that.

And his mate said, "Charley, leave the thing there and they'll think it's a skunk!"

BRISTOL

A SPECIAL session of Somerset County Council was summoned to deal with two highway employees who had painted a white line over a dead badger lying in the middle of the highway.

With that same "get-up-and-go" exhibited by couch-bound men with TV remotes, this dynamic duo — whose job it was to paint white lines down the middle of the road — came across the defunct badger and painted right over it.

A traveling salesman spotted the painted badger while driving along the highway, took photographs and sent them to the local newspaper.

If Loudon Wainwright III doesn't milk a song out of this, something stinks.

Woman without sense of humor ends relationship with man without brain

LONDON

A 21-YEAR-OLD university student was dumped by his girlfriend — just because he got married while on a backpacking trip to the United States. The 3rd year economics major was puzzled, saying he hoped she would understand.

The young man explained that while traveling about America, he ended up in Las Vegas where, after a night of gambling and drinking (and drinking and gambling), he proposed to a young Australian woman he had just met in a casino. Next — and as nearly as he can remember — off they went to the Candlelight Chapel.

The spontaneous though silly stunt over and done with, the two parted company the next day, he flying home to England, his bride to Australia, each of them armed with a wacky adventure story to tell their friends.

When the fellow told his parents, his father laughed, though his mother cried. But when he told his girlfriend, she failed to see the humor in it and declared their relationship through.

"Hey, you hear about it all the time. You go to Vegas, you gamble, you drink, you get married. It's funny, right?"

But I have a letter from my parents — wouldn't you like to see it?

CLUJ, ROMANIA

A TEENAGE boy is in deep doo-doo after police discovered that he attempted to hire the services of a prostitute with counterfeit money he produced on his home computer.

His would-be companion, however, flagged down police after determining that several of the playboy's bills had identical serial numbers.

Police said the enterprising youngster was also armed with several fake bus tickets and a bogus doctor's note excusing him from school for the day.

Young Demetrius has *a lot of 'splainin' to do,* as they say in Romania.

I distinctly said, "Extra dry, on the rocks, with a twist, and hold the bacon!"

LA CUARTA, CHILE

WHILE there was no official reaction from the bride-to-be, the wedding was indefinitely postponed while her 27-year-old fiancé recovered in hospital from a stag party which witnesses claim was, "wilder than Maradona's birthday party."

"First the young man was stripped naked and spanked," reports show. "Then there were performances by 4 strippers hired for the occasion, and a collection of porn movies, and much drinking."

At some point in the evening, the man's friends told doctors they mixed him an "atomic cocktail," containing rum, margarine, mustard — and bacon — then cheered him on while the man slurped it down from a wash basin.

Doctors said the man slipped into oblivion after demolishing the bowl of booze and was rushed to hospital by friends.

Speaking on behalf of the man's betrothed, a friend said she is naturally disappointed, and that no, there would not be a second stag party to celebrate the official wedding, whenever that might be.

First I take Manhattan . . . then I take you, my little Fräulein

HAMBURG

STORMING a house after concerned neighbors reported the sounds of gunfire in the night, a special forces squad found a buxom, semi-clad young woman and her equally underdressed boyfriend shooting at one another from opposite ends of the room.

Relieved, and more than a little red-faced, the police confiscated the weapons — and the blanks — and left the pair to finish their evening.

"It was the boyfriend's idea of a sex game," police explained. "Apparently, the gunfight is his favorite way to get excited."

The 28-year-old woman and her 27-year-old lover were not named — or charged.

One neighbor in the affluent neighborhood of this German city told investigating officers that her attention was aroused when she heard loud moaning and groaning following an extended burst of gunfire.

Being in love means never having to say you're stupid

LISBON

IT weighed 62 pounds, measured over 40 inches in diameter, contained 518 red roses — one for every day they'd been apart — and the *Guinness Book of World Records* calls it "the largest bouquet of roses ever sold by a florist in one order."

The love-struck suitor — intent on a grand gesture, it seems — had originally planned to deliver his aromatic apology by helicopter, but foul weather intervened and the flowers had to be delivered by hand.

The couple, said friends, had been dating for approximately 3 years.

No matter.

Whatever it was that caused the breakup is anyone's guess, but rumors suggest that the problem weighed no more than 115 pounds, measured approximately 36-22-35, and may or may not have received 1 red rose for the 1 night they spent together.

All said, the little lady said "No," and the bozo with the giant bouquet ends up in this book too.

Well, he did eat all my bait, the propeller off the boat, and quite a bit of tackle before I finally landed him

TORONTO

THERE'S nothing men love more than a little bit of fishing and some good ol' fashion competition. So when the stakes are high, it's not surprising that the combination of the two can get downright weighty.

Take the Ontario angler who was charged with fraud after stuffing lead filings down the gullet of a salmon in an attempt to win a $10,000 fishing-derby prize.

Organizers of the *Great Salmon Hunt* — sponsored by *The Toronto Sun* — said the scaly little devil ground up about 7 ½ pounds of lead pipe then stuffed it into the fish before taking his "34-pounder" to the weigh station.

Police were called when weigh-in officials concluded there was something very fishy about his catch of the day.

Not if you're wearing that same shirt and underwear, we're not . . .

LONDON

MORE than 30% of male soccer fans say they don't have sex on the night before important games, indicates a poll conducted in England prior to the 2002 World Cup.

We think we know why.

Although socks weren't mentioned, 45% of the men surveyed claimed to wear the same "lucky" shirt before every big game, and close to 5% of those claimed they never washed their shirts while their team was on a winning streak.

One super-fan said he won't wash his underwear throughout the entire month-long series.

The poll asked 3,000 British soccer fans about their superstitions. The pollsters, no doubt, insist that their results are accurate in 19 out of 20 marriages, 4 out of 5 times . . . or whatever.

I'm wearing a blue pantsuit with a silver badge and really shiny, black boots

VIENNA

IN yet another attempt to walk while chewing gum, a 32-year-old Austrian actually gave his home phone number to a woman who said she'd love to listen to his heavy breathing, but was too busy at that moment and would have to call him back later.

The woman then made a call of her own — to local authorities.

The dirty dialer later admitted to police that his hobby involved placing hundreds of calls every week — to phone numbers chosen at random from the Vienna phone book.

And Freud was an Austrian?

Where there's a Jane and a Spot, there's bound to be a Dick, right?

GOTHENBURG, SWEDEN

A 29-YEAR-OLD Swede is taking his ex-girlfriend to court and suing her for visitation rights — to a dog.

The young man claims that he and his ex bought the dog together, and ever since the breakup has not been allowed to see "his best friend."

The unnamed Scandinavian says he will call several witnesses to testify that he paid half the cost of the pooch and all the animal's veterinary care.

The man has told court officials that if he loses his suit for visitation rights, he wants half the initial price paid for the dog — with interest.

LOOKING BACK ON IT, WE SHOULDA HAD THE ANCHOVIES

BOSTON

THEIR holdup of a local pizza parlor went exactly as planned, but as the robbers were about to flee with the dough, Johnny Ortega and Mikey Cordova couldn't believe their ears: police sirens were wailing toward them. But hey, no problemo.

Quicker than you can say double cheese, pepperoni, green pepper, and onions, they came up with an idea.

"Now listen you, and listen good," Johnny said, untying the shop employee he had just earlier bound up with duct tape.

"You tie me and Mikey up so it looks like we work here, and when the cops come in you tell 'em the crooks ran out the back door."

Quick thinking, or what?

The employee, having been taught never to argue with a customer, trussed up the two armed men before it occurred to either of them that there might be something terribly wrong with the picture.

At the scene of the crime, Mikey and Johnny were bound up so tightly that it took police about 10 minutes to set them free — so they could be put in cuffs.

Asked about his time with Britney, he said he found her a bit stiff and difficult to talk to

SIOUX LOOKOUT, ONTARIO

WHETHER he hoped that neighbors might see them entering his house together, or that someone might report having seen her with him, police won't speculate.

What they will say is that their 3-day search for a life-sized, promotional cutout of Britney Spears came to a peaceful end thanks in no small part to media interest in her mysterious disappearance.

Publicity surrounding the pop diva's missing merchandising prop alerted residents in this northern Ontario community to be on the lookout for the life-size replica. According to one of the officers assigned to the case, an alert citizen called to report seeing Britney standing demurely in the window of a neighbor's home.

Officers say a young man at that address claimed he'd taken her home after finding her alone on a street corner in the middle of town.

All's well that ends well.

At last report, Britney was back at work beside the soft drink dispenser at the local Gas Bar. Police say no charges will be laid.

Hell, if you'll sign my pledge card, I'll see that everybody gets a drink

LAMBERTVILLE, NEW JERSEY

EVEN at the peak of a season-long, state-wide drought, New Jersey police were skeptical when a man they caught running naked across a bridge explained he was only doing so to make it rain.

According to officers at the scene, the 33-year-old — running on 40-proof octane — at first attempted to flee when officers approached him midway across the Lambertville-New Hope Bridge. He soon gave up.

Minutes later, curled under a blanket in the rear seat of the cruiser, the man claimed his naked run would bring rain — "lots of rain — to the entire state!"

Police drove the juiced-up jogger to headquarters where he was given a chance to dry out.

There must be 50 ways to kidnap your mother . . .

TAMPICO, MEXICO

CONCERNED he didn't have enough money for his wedding, a 21-year-old talked his fiancée into helping him kidnap his own mother in the hope that a $1 million ransom would pay for the kind of wedding that he and his bride-to-be had always dreamed of.

Newspapers report that the fellow — and his best man — burst into his 63-year-old mother's home, bound and gagged her, and then tossed her into the trunk of a car.

According to police, the duo then drove to a nearby hotel where the man's girlfriend was already phoning relatives in an attempt to collect the money.

After tracing the phone calls, officers arrested the man and his fiancée at the hotel, but released them almost immediately when the mother refused to press charges. The best man, police said, has not been located.

Citing family ties, the lady told police that she did not want to press charges.

But wait 'til your father hears about this, young man.

"And she hands us a stack of fifties, so my buddy says 'Don't you have anything smaller?'"

ATLANTA

THE dream of stealing more money than they could possibly carry turned into a nightmare for a dimwitted duo who robbed a highway tollbooth without stopping to wonder how much 2,000 quarters might weigh.

That was their first mistake, according to police officers called to the scene.

Their second mistake was choosing a garbage bag to carry the loot.

Tollbooth operators say the garbage bag split as the two men dragged it toward a getaway car they'd parked nearby, leaving a silver trail of coins across the highway and along the shoulder of the road.

The following day, while checking out a stolen car several miles from the crime scene, police found $70 worth of change scattered throughout the vehicle, and set to dusting the car for prints.

"I hope they saved a couple of coins to call a lawyer," one cop said.

I don't understand . . . Santa Claus makes it look so #%&#@% easy

WESTPORT, NEW ZEALAND

POLICE didn't have far to go when a neighbor called to report someone breaking into a building across the street.

The building across the street was the Granity Jail near Westport and, sure enough, the guy was already locked up inside.

The recently-closed jail had been used briefly as a temporary residence for a member of the local police force and his family.

A police spokesperson said the family had moved out the day before the break-in and had removed all their belongings, with the exception of a cell-full of toys which the constable's wife had been collecting for a daycare center.

With nothing else of value on the premises, the 38-year-old burglar was filling his rucksack with toys when the door of the cell apparently closed — and then locked behind him.

HO, HO, HO!

Once upon a time there was a really dumb holdup man who looked like . . . this

SILVER SPRING, MARYLAND

FIRST he had his passport photo taken while he cased the joint.

Then he pulled out his gun and demanded that the young photographer empty her cash into his tote bag.

Then he grabbed the photo she had just taken and fled down the street.

Then the young lady dialed 911 while she took the negative from her camera and printed several dozen copies for police.

Then the police distributed the photos to every police officer in Silver Spring.

Okay, go to sleep now and I'll read you the rest tomorrow night.

"Australian Rules" just about explains everything, doesn't it?

PORT MELBOURNE

OFFICIALS suspended an Australian Rules Football player for 10 games after he bit an opponent's doo-dad during a match between Port Melbourne and Springvale.

Doctors say the injured player's privates were bruised and he lost a small amount of blood.

Apologizing for the bite, the suspended player said he chomped down instinctively when his face became smothered during a pile-up.

"It was a split second decision," he claimed, while accepting the league's ruling that he will have to undergo counseling before being allowed to play again.

In another unseemly account of a footy player trying making his way up from downunder, it was reported that the National Rugby League handed out a 12-week suspension to a player for poking a finger up an opponent's . . .

Darn, we wuz hoping she'd wed one of them insider trading fellas . . .

York, Pennsylvania

WHEN the court clerk asked the 30-year-old groom to provide his occupation for the marriage license he was seeking, he replied "criminal."

The exchange took place in the basement of the county courthouse prior to the wedding of a convicted armed robber and the mother of his 2 children. No family or friends attended the brief ceremony.

"That was a joke. Did they write that down?" asked the holdup man who was attended by sheriff's deputies throughout the ceremonial vows.

"Well, he is a criminal," muttered County Sheriff Bill Hose who was also in attendance.

If they're not a bitin' or a pokin' they're stealing cars

SYDNEY, AUSTRALIA

AFTER a high-speed chase through city streets, police arrested a man who stole a taxi from a cabby who refused to let him into his car.

Incidentally, the man was wearing a bikini and wielding a leather bullwhip.

The driver told police he refused the fare because of the way the man was dressed.

Police said the taxi company's GPS tracking system helped them follow the stolen vehicle.

That's the story, reported in Australian newspapers in a style and tone that newspapers around the world generally use when reporting the weather.

What is it with Australians — the weather, the island mentality, or simply the fact that they spend their entire lifetimes standing upside-down?

In the good ol' days, he'd have worn a garter belt and we never would have caught him

MERRIAM, MISSOURI

POLICE say a man suspected of robbing at least 3 local shops while wearing pantyhose over his head might still be at large had he stuck to light-colored stockings.

After a successful robbery of a doll shop while disguised in gray tights, the man switched to dark-black pantyhose, then robbed a convenience store. But while fleeing the scene the very short-sighted burglar ran headfirst into a garbage dumpster, spilling cash and cigarettes all over the parking lot.

The man was still on his hands and knees, scooping up the loot when police arrived.

The man's wife — provider of the tights and driver of the getaway car — was also charged at the scene.

Opening Monday at a laundromat near you . . .

SANTA MONICA

SAYING it has absolutely nothing to do with revenge, a California man celebrated his divorce by writing, directing, starring in, and financing a $1.5 million tell-all musical comedy about his marriage.

Singing and dancing his way through the ups and downs — from first kiss to first base, from the opening pitch to the last out of the game — the divorcee claims the whole thing was done to help his daughter understand the complexities of married life.

Repeatedly asked if "Divorce: The Musical" is not tantamount to airing his family's laundry in public, the fellow is adamant in his denials.

"I didn't do this to get even," he insists.

When approached, his ex-wife said she'd read the book and had no plans to take in the flick.

Forgive me Father for I have sinned, am sinning, and just might sin again

OTTAWA

A 72-YEAR-OLD retired priest suffered a fatal heart attack while relaxing in a private room at a Quebec strip club near Ottawa.

Neither the young dancer who had performed for him, nor staffers at the club were able to revive the elderly cleric before an ambulance whisked him off to hospital where he was pronounced dead on arrival.

Patrons at the club said he appeared to be enjoying himself before deciding to join one of the performers for a private audience — in the club's dimly lit "Champagne Lounge."

Police later arrested 11 people at the popular club, saying a former dancer had confessed that some of the ladies were supplementing their income by offering selected customers a little taste of heaven.

Amen, and goodnight.

Okay, this time I'll pretend that I'm in jail and you pretend that you're the guard

EDMONTON

PRETENDING to be a police officer, a 35-year-old Edmonton man got himself arrested while trying to get free sex from an undercover policewoman pretending to be a prostitute.

Sex trade workers told police (real ones) that this scaly scam artist had been visiting their strutting grounds for several nights, and may even have duped one or more of the young women workers before hitting on the curvaceous copper.

Police say that on the night in question, the randy lothario with the empty wallet even flashed phony police ID at the lady cop, suggesting that he wouldn't arrest her if she treated him to a sampling of her wares.

It was at this point that the undercover officer signaled her backup and — before he could mutter "thigh-high boots and stiletto heels" — two detectives emerged from a nearby doorway and arrested the imposter on the spot.

Ooowee, look, there's Naomi Campbell and there's Robert Downey Jr., and . . . Hey! Isn't that Don Knotts?

RIO DE JANEIRO

THE sneak preview of a film about drug dealers got more media attention than anyone could have ever hoped when a man reputed to be one of the city's top drug lords crashed a black-tie reception for invited guests and got himself arrested.

Astonished guests at director Fernando Meirelles' *Cidade de Deus* (City of God) could be excused for smelling a publicity stunt, but the bust was real, the cuffs were real, and the cops hustling their suspect into a waiting cruiser were the real McCoy.

Like a moth to candlelight, police suspect it was the lure of the bright lights that lured the starry-eyed bandit out of the shadows and into a spotlight he now regrets.

"Curiosity has once more killed *o gato*," said an officer at the scene.

AND WHAT ABOUT LEAVING THE TOILET SEAT UP...? RUN THAT ONE BY ME AGAIN

STOCKHOLM

AMONG the many things that women will never understand, some men will tell you, is the uselessness of
maps when driving in strange cities, Monday Night
Football . . . or even why a man might crawl into a foul-
smelling garbage chute to rescue a moth-eaten sweater that his
wife thoughtlessly and inexplicably tossed into the trash.

"I am quite small," the man explained to his rescuers,
describing how he had attempted to retrieve the sweater by
climbing feet-first into his apartment's narrow garbage chute.

"I mean I knew the garbage would be hauled away early
next morning, so I really had no choice."

The rescue of the sweater, according to both the man and
his bewildered wife, was going swimmingly until, somewhere
between floors, the 25-year-old man became stuck.

After several hours, rescue of the poor chap was turned
over to firefighters called to the scene when the fellow's wife
was unable to hoist him out of the chute using a hastily built
rope of knotted bed sheets.

The hand-knit, black and gray beauty, had been tossed out
by his wife, apparently unaware of the enormous sentimental
value of its frayed hem, the holes in the elbows, or the fact
that it had been knit by his mother.

The sweater, the man recently told neighbors, is now back
where it belongs — on the floor of the couple's bedroom.

"That's my story, and I'm sticking to it."

TOKYO

A SAKE-SWILLING university professor ended up in court after bar owners called police to report that the man had stripped off his clothes and was riding one of his female students like a pony.

Asked to explain his behavior, the bareback-riding brainiac claimed that he and his student were recreating a famous equestrian statue.

"It was art. We were making art!" the man exclaimed in court.

The judge may not have known much about art, but he knew what he liked, and he didn't like the picture painted by several witnesses.

The man was fined 330,000 Japanese Yen.

Adding insult to injury, the poodle didn't like him either

FRANKFURT

A GERMAN pensioner has sued a dating agency saying it not only charged him a small fortune, but provided but one date in the more than two months he subscribed to its services.

To make matters worse, claimed the 65-year-old gentleman, the one woman the agency sent his way spent the entire evening petting and brushing and talking to her pet poodle while ignoring him totally.

"She also smoked — like a chimney!" he added.

The man said he paid over $2,000 to the introduction service after reading an advertisement that promised he would meet all kinds of lonely, and lovely ladies.

"For that, I get a visit from a woman and a dog."

Life in the fast lane, the mysteries of folk medicine, and the one-fingered salute

TORONTO

AS the morning-after police blotters attest the world over, holidays bring out the best and the worst in everyone.

Wrapping up their July 1 Canada Day weekend in Toronto, police reported that they:

1. stopped a man for driving erratically, discovered that his feet were wrapped in banana skins (to cure bunions, he explained) while a large bloodhound in the passenger seat (without a seatbelt) nibbled and licked the man's ear as he sped along the highway;

2. arrested another hoser for tossing a one-fingered salute at an unmarked cruiser, discovered that the driver had no insurance, and that his license was already under suspension for a previous offence;

3. answered a trucker's complaint that some lunatic had just sped by with his underwear proudly draped across the dashboard of his car while celebrating the excitement of the holiday weekend in a *very* personal manner.

The weekend totals for the Toronto area — 148 people charged with aggressive driving, 31 people for driving without insurance, 21 for driving without a license, 39 people charged with seatbelt offences, and 6 charged with operating a motor vehicle while impaired.

Total number of women drivers in the above tally — zero.

I'm afraid
It's not your
money, chump, it's you

MANCHESTER

A RETIRED traffic warden who won close to $400,000 in the National Lottery, was fined $200 for harassment after mailing a copy of the prize check to his ex-girlfriend with a "HA! HA!" note attached.

Dumped just weeks before his big win, this loser's idea of revenge did not amuse the court.

In addition to the fine, the judge levied a restraining order and a warning that if the man even attempted to contact his former sweetie again, he would end up in jail for at least 6 months.

Evidence showed that until his windfall, the 54-year-old bachelor got his jollies by repeatedly badgering the young lady with silent phone calls.

Richer, but deep down inside as shallow as ever, the poor clown said he thought his winnings would win back the lady's attention.

And what did the lady say to his newfound wealth: "Get lost!"

Don't wait! Fill out the attached subscription form today — you could be a winner!

GREENSBURG, PENNSYLVANIA

A 37-YEAR-OLD inmate earned himself extra prison time after sending dozens of phony magazine subscriptions to relatives scheduled to testify against him at an upcoming trial.

Angry with his estranged wife and a score of other relatives, the man forged their names onto the subscription cards from every magazine in the prison library.

"There were tons of them," the assistant district attorney told the court. "Enough to fill dozens of mailboxes."

Accepting the fellow's plea of guilty to fraudulently subscribing to *Penthouse, Maxim Hustler*, the *National Enquirer* and dozens of other magazines, the judge added another 23 months to the man's existing 10-year prison term.

Why can't he be normal and hang around the mall like the other kids?

NORTH WILDWOOD, NEW JERSEY

A 17-YEAR-OLD budding break-in artist was charged with burglary and theft when police found him hanging around the scene of the crime.

Officers said they found the young man dangling helplessly from the top of a roll-up door on a concession stand during a routine night patrol of downtown neighborhoods.

"Police don't know if he got tangled up while breaking in, or whether it happened as he was leaving the premises," said a juvenile court spokesperson. "But somehow his baggy, hip-hop trousers became snagged on a metal hook and he was just hanging there looking real dumb when they found him."

And for my next trick, I will attempt to unswallow the sword

HAMILTON, ONTARIO

IN what his girlfriend described as a "drunken accident from hell," a 33-year-old daredevil ended up in hospital after attempting to swallow a friend's 40-inch-long sword.

Witnesses say the fellow had managed to swallow about ¾ of the weapon when things went terribly wrong.

The man was rushed to hospital where he was treated for a collapsed lung, a cut throat and damage to his voice box.

A very dumb stunt, according to his girlfriend.

"I mean, I love him and all," she said, "but what a jerk!"

Proof positive once again that men know everything there is to know

FRANKFURT

A 21-YEAR-OLD German talked his 18-year-old girl-friend into hiding in the restroom of a bedding shop until closing time — so they could test the water beds. Police said the couple waited until the last employee left the store before bouncing passionately from one bed to another.

After several hours of comparative shopping, the couple left the building only to trigger the alarm.

Officers said the young woman was convinced that her boyfriend had planned their adventure very carefully and that nothing could possibly go wrong.

But as the couple attempted to leave the shop, they activated the alarm on an emergency exit.

"I thought he knew what he was doing," the young lady told police who arrived on the scene. "But can you believe the blockhead, he was still telling me nothing could go wrong while the policeman was cuffing him."

Dimwitted Animal?
Dumb Ass?
Dyslexic Amateur?

FOCSANI, ROMANIA

SOME men are indeed dumber than others. So it's not surprising that the guy who gave his wife jewelry engraved with his mistress's initials was not so fast on his feet.

"M.D.," he could have said, staring lovingly into her eyes. "Why, that stands for *My Dearest*, of course. What else?"

But not this clown whose stuttered and mumbled explanation was so lame that he ended up in hospital when his wife knocked him unconscious with a marble ashtray.

Police were called to the scene by neighbors who reported screaming, shouting and wailing coming from a house in the normally quiet neighborhood.

Whether the man's mistress figured out the meaning of the initials D.A. dangling from her gold necklace is anyone's guess.

Will George come back to Helen? Will Helen leave John and join the nunnery? Tune in tomorrow for the next episode of . . .

SACCLE, ROMANIA

A28-YEAR-OLD Romanian ended up in hospital when his wife's boyfriend punched him in the nose because he wasn't doing his fair share of housework.

The woman's lover told police that the fight broke out over the sharing of household chores — dusting, doing the dishes, vacuuming, that kind of thing.

"He just got lazy," the young man complained. "He didn't do anything all day."

Police say the boyfriend moved into the couple's home — and the wife's bedroom — a year ago, forcing the husband to move out onto a cot halfway down the hall.

At last report, the woman was living alone while her husband remained in hospital with a ruptured ego.

The boyfriend was nowhere to be found.

Though upset that his wife did not defend him during the fracas, the husband said he would move back into this matrimonial snake pit as soon as he recovered from his injuries.

"I love my wife," he told friends. "That's all I can say."

Scissors cut paper, rock crushes scissors, and croquet mallet cracks cranium

CALGARY

PROVING once again that real guys can turn anything to their disadvantage, a men's softball team traded insults with a men's croquet team in a Calgary athletic field and learned the hard way that football and hockey aren't necessarily the toughest games in town.

According to police reports, what started out as name calling between surly softballers and wily wicketers quickly turned into a shouting match.

The shouting match, say witnesses, turned into a brawl and the brawl, in turn, became a mallet-swinging, head-banging, free-for-all.

Final score: 7 injured, 3 hauled off to hospital, and 1 guy seriously injured.

Rumors that Canada's Sports Network shelved plans for a full-contact curling special in favor of an Australian Rules croquet match could not be confirmed.

And then he said, "Well now little lady, let's see if you can swim"

VIENNA

AUSTRIAN police in patrol boats combed the waters of Lake Constance for 20 minutes after a frantic weekend boater called to report a corpse floating in the water.

Distraught tourists and worried locals traded gossip as they watched searchers and rescue teams criss-cross the waters of the lake bordering Switzerland and Germany.

A boating accident?

A careless swimmer?

Someone thrown overboard by an angry lover?

None of the above.

Local papers reported that police finally located the bobbing body which turned out to be a cast-off, inflatable female sex doll.

Somewhat deflated, the "young lady" was last seen in the company of one of her rescuers.

Dr. Doolittle goes to Romania

BUCHAREST

ANGERED by his wife's collection of fur coats and wraps, a 40-year-old Romanian carried out a personal, one-man, anti-fur protest — by marching up and down the sidewalk in front of his home to both the dismay — and delight of his neighbors.

"I'm totally fed up with her hobby of buying fur garments," he told the crowd gathered to witness the spectacle.

"I don't know what it is with these women," he shouted. "My wife has 5 fur coats, and goodness knows how many hats, collars and sets of gloves made from the fur of other helpless animals. The next thing you know, she'll be wearing fur underwear."

Saying they had no intention of pressing charges, police quickly disbursed the noisy and prurient onlookers while the man's wife and several neighbors helped the hapless fellow back into his house.

He remembers a time when everyone knew their neighbors, and things like this just didn't happen

BREDA, HOLLAND

COMING home to a house that has been broken into can be an unnerving experience.

Most people call the police after a quick visual inventory and making certain that the intruder is not still on the scene.

And this, police said, is exactly what a 33-year-old professional burglar did when some sleazy, dirty, rotten, despicable, sneak thief made off with some of his favorite possessions while he was hard at work in another part of town.

Police say the man reported the break-in before considering that almost every room in his house was filled with furniture, art, and knick-knacks stolen from other homes and businesses in the area.

Entering the man's home, one policeman spotted a computer still bearing a sticker from a local school. Another officer pointed to several paintings reported stolen months prior.

And a third policeman read the flustered break-in artist his rights while checking off a half dozen items on his stolen-goods list.

Perhaps we could call him Eduardo … Mr. Eduardo, like that guy on TV

ROME

AS soon as the boy was born, the proud poppa knew exactly what he'd name him — "Varenne Giampaolo," after one of the most famous racehorses in Italy.

And son of a gun, didn't he forget to mention this to his wife.

Now, of course, the courts are involved.

Upon learning that her husband had sneaked off to the city records office while she was still in hospital, the woman immediately challenged the naming of the child, saying she had already selected "Christian."

"She says a horse's name is embarrassing and insulting," said a court official.

The husband is equally adamant, claiming that Varenne Giampaolo is no ordinary horse: "He is a national hero in Italy . . . athlete of the year in 2001!

And the winner is . . .

Stop me before I drop my driver's license and my passport again . . .

CARMEL, CALIFORNIA

TALK about making a police detective's day. Cops are looking for a holdup man who walked into a local bank in downtown Carmel and handed the teller a note demanding money. He carefully explained he wanted the kind that had no exploding traceable dye — and if the teller knew what was good for her, she would make no attempt to trigger the alarm.

The man then walked out with the cash, but while in the process of stuffing the loot into a backpack, he dropped his driver's license.

Police have the name and address of the heist meister, whose ID describes him as 43-years-old, 6 foot 2, with green eyes and brown hair.

A spokesperson for the Carmel police department said that if more proof is required, the description on the license matches the footage from the bank's surveillance cameras.

I know what you're thinking punk. You're asking yourself, do they have five clues or six?

The one thing he was very firm about . . . he won't do windows

CAMDEN, ARKANSAS

SURE they're dirty jobs, but somebody's gotta do them!

Police in this Arkansas town 100 miles south of Little Rock are on the lookout for a handyman with a two-track mind.

According to at least a half-dozen callers, an enterprising young fellow has been going door-to-door through several neighborhoods offering to clean septic tanks — in exchange for sex.

Police say the fact that the description of the man is so similar to that of other calls they've been receiving, they suspect he's the same guy who's been canvassing other neighborhoods offering to clean their sewer systems — in exchange for guns.

And if he turns out to be the other end of the horse, she'll have no-one to blame but herself

LINCOLNSHIRE, ENGLAND

HE played the front end, she played the rear, and like a story out of Hollywood they made beautiful *mooosic* together.

"It was love at first sight," said Sharon Colley, who played the back half of "Daisy," the cow in their drama club's production of *Babes in the Wood*.

Kevin Blackburn, who played the front (or horny end), said it didn't matter to him where Sharon was when he met her. "We spent a lot of time rehearsing and I found her to be the perfect package."

And *udderly* beautiful, according to other members of the drama club.

Ms. Colley told friends that she joined the troupe to do hair and makeup and had not planned to join the cast until someone offered her the part.

The duo has a cast of five children from previous roles.

So far, not even a postcard or a phone call, so we're still in the dark . . .

FORT WORTH

A COUPLE of Texans, a snootful of booze, and an argument about who's going to heaven and who's going to hell was settled with a shotgun blast that sent one man winging (or sliding) into the next world, and the other fellow off to jail.

Having spent the night bar-hopping with friends, the two decided on a couple more drinks before calling it a night. According to witnesses, the men were sitting around a picnic table in a trailer park when a religious argument got downright personal.

Apparently frustrated by the see-saw debate and eager to settle the argument over which one of them was bound for heaven (and which for hell) the one man grabbed a loaded shotgun and threatened to shoot himself, which, of course, would have determined the course of debate once and for all.

His drinking partner, however, took exception, and shouting "If you wanna shoot somebody, then shoot me," began a struggle over the gun. The gun went off and he was killed instantly.

. . . and we'll never know.

And do you, Rosie, promise to love, honor, and cherish Jason for at least a couple of hours?

DETROIT

YOU'D think that after dating her for 14 months, a fellow would have a pretty good read on the woman of his dreams. Well, here's a guy who got it wrong, wrong, wrong.

The man in question, a 34-year-old sportswriter, claimed his blushing bride began acting "cool" toward him about an hour after they exchanged vows.

Adding insult to injury, the 35-year-old bride wouldn't sit beside him at the wedding party brunch.

Furthermore, he claims, she absolutely refused to sit at his table for dinner that night.

"She told me that the act of getting married made her realize she couldn't get married." The groom then told friends that by the end of the 5th hour of their married life, his new bride knew it was never meant to be.

So he dumped her, right?

Not quite. The young heartbreaker insisted that it would be a terrible waste of money if they were to scrap their honeymoon plans.

So hell-bent on winning himself a spot in this book, off they went.

Okay, that's double cheese, pepperoni, mushrooms, and hold the anchovies

STRATFORD, ONTARIO

BRAIN surgeons and astronauts, hell even book publishers will tell you that the trouble with memorizing phone numbers is the likelihood that sooner or later you'll dial one when you mean to dial the other.

Take 411 and 911 and the 49-year-old guy in this sleepy little town who dialed 911 and promptly hung up when he realized his mistake.

As police always do when 911 is dialed, a patrol car was immediately dispatched to the man's address. During a cursory search of the house — to make certain all was as well as it appeared to be — officers discovered a sizeable marijuana farm in the basement, and immediately charged the occupant with production and possession.

Hope he knows that if the guards don't bring him his pizza in 30 minutes, he's free.

Did you guys ever notice that the word "police" is "ecilop" spelled backwards?

CLEVELAND

SPOTTING a truck parked in the lot of a downtown bar with its engine idling and its lights on, police arrested a man asleep at the wheel — a half-bag of marijuana in his lap and a half-rolled joint in his yellowed fingers.

Arresting officers say the man woke up when they opened the truck door, a half-crooked smile on his face, a half-baked thought at the edge of his mind.

"Hey, guys, wuz up" was his only response.

Police say the fellow, who had obviously fallen asleep while rolling himself a late night smack, was wakened by the flash of the camera they used to photograph him at the time of his arrest.

How about
"Loudest Screaming While Having a Red Hot Poker..." or something like that

BOMBAY

A N Indian martial arts instructor has recently claimed the record for . . . having the most cement blocks smashed on his groin with a sledgehammer.

A *Guinness Book of World Records* spokesperson said Bibhuti Nayak had three 41-pound cement blocks smashed on his groin at one time, thereby bettering, by one, the current "groin break" record held by American Cliff Flenoy.

Mr. Nayak claims he set his sights on the groin-break record after watching a television special on human endurance.

"These performances are not only strenuous," explained the 36-year-old, "but also dangerous."

Mr. Nayak is already mentioned in India's *Limca Book of Records* for managing 1,448 sit-ups in an hour and, for the more heroic feat of getting kicked in the groin — 43 times.

Despite the danger, Nayak says he is already thinking about newer, tougher, dumber records to set.

And before you could say "wash, rinse, spin, dry" there he was, naked as the day he was born

MADISON, WISCONSIN

TWO female customers complained to police after a naked man in a 24-hour laundromat tossed his clothes into a dryer, then pulled up a chair beside them and started up a conversation.

According to witnesses, the young man sat talking with the ladies for several minutes until they began laughing.

Upset or unnerved, the fellow tore his clothes from the dryer, quickly dressed and then ran off down the street.

Asked if they would be willing to attend a police lineup, the ladies told officers they doubted they'd be able to recognize him — with his clothes on.

DON'T ASK

Mebane, North Carolina

STAFFERS at a supermarket called police when they became suspicious of a small, late-model truck circling the parking lot in front of their store, fearing that what they were witnessing might well be the preliminaries to a robbery attempt.

Each time the truck made its way around the lot, they noted, it would pull up in front of the store, park there for a minute or two, then speed off.

Police said the driver of the truck led them on a brief chase around the parking lot at speeds of up to 40-miles-per-hour before surrendering.

Inside the vehicle, police discovered a naked man who had smeared himself liberally, all over, everywhere, from top to bottom and head to toe — with Vaseline. Turns out, the suspect was not so easily apprehended.

Mary Margaret Flanagan! It's me, Tom Behan . . . Sister Mary Theresa's class! I sat behind you

BELFAST

IF there's a list of qualities least likely to come in handy when robbing banks, 'tis pretty certain that friendliness and sociability come awful close to the top of it, now wouldn't you say?

Tell this to the 33-year-old Dubliner cooling his duff in the hoosegow after his first ever attempt at robbing banks.

Herding the tellers into the manager's office just after opening, he was, when faith and beggorra, in walks a tardy teller who had just stopped for tea on her way to work.

Squinting through the eyeholes of his balaclava, the fellow couldn't believe his Irish eyes.

"Late again Flanagan! Late again!" he sings out loud.

And there's something about that joke and that laugh which reminds her of how the boys teased her back in school.

"Blabbermouth Behan!" she shouts at him. "You better get out of here if you know what's good for you!"

And so he did, running straight into a passing constable before he had time to remove his mask.

HE'S CUTE AS A BUTTON, TIDY AROUND THE HOUSE, AND ANSWERS TO "DUMBO"

OTTAWA

CONCERNED about marriages of convenience — and abuse of the country's immigration regulations — an Ottawa judge rejected a man's application for citizenship when the man and his wife failed a quickie quiz — about each other.

Asked how much they paid for their car, the couple's answers were thousands of dollars apart.

Asked what they did on Christmas day, the pair's answers were as far apart as the opposite ends of an 18-pound turkey.

When it came to the practice of birth control, the judge was left to wonder if they slept in the same bed, the same room, or the same town.

"Condoms," the woman answered quickly.

"She's on the pill," said her beau.

"Not even close," the judge said, shaking his head in disbelief, and told the dolt to pack his bags for the next flight home.

Carlos cannot come to the phone just now, how you say in English, he is tied up

RIO DE JANEIRO

IN Brazil where kidnapping is said to be as common as infidelity, it's no surprise to discover that practitioners of the latter have turned to the former as one more subterfuge in their on-going search for the perfect woman.

Officers in several cities say that unfaithful husbands have been showing up at police stations the morning after midnight trysts claiming they have just escaped after being held overnight against their wills.

At least 5 "kidnappings" already reported this year have involved men who lied to police and were subsequently charged with making a false report.

Counting the hole
in his head, some would say,
you get a total of 172

OMAHA

EYEING a spot in the *Guinness Book of World Records,* a 21-year-old university student walked into a body piercing parlor and emerged hours later with 171 new holes in his body, thereby laying claim to the most body piercings ever obtained in one day.

That, say the folks who meticulously track such demonstrations of human endurance, breaks the previous world record by a grand total of 28 holes.

Reports reveal that 10 of the day's piercings were made along the man's collarbone, the rest were in his arms.

Operators of the body piercing parlor where the new record was set say they had been searching for the past 10 years for the kind of man who could endure that kind of pain.

Saying the stunt was all his idea, the man's 19-year-old girlfriend said she was, yes, "very proud of him."

And for an all-expenses paid weekend in Sudbury, I will see that you are rewarded with a C-minus . . .

TORONTO

A PART-TIME instructor at a city college was tossed off campus following complaints that he was blackmailing students with a good-marks-for-good-money scam.

Police said the 36-year-old math teacher promised students an A+ in return for airline tickets or cash.

Newspaper reports indicate the man hounded students who were doing badly in his math classes, promising them top marks if they would go along with his plan.

The students, obviously intent on getting an education the old-fashioned way, refused his offer and reported him to college administrators, who in turn called police.

What? This old thing? Gosh, I've had it for as long as I can remember

FORT LAUDERDALE

FLORIDA police say an arrest made at a rock concert was a simple matter of what's "in" and what's "out" in the fashion world.

According to officers on the scene, the old rocker showed up wearing a bright orange, prison-issue jumpsuit. When questioned, he admitted he had recently been a guest of the state, and simply "forgot" to return the jumpsuit when he was released.

"The kids wear anything to these concerts, real wild stuff, but he kinda stood out in the crowd with that 'Polk County Jail' stenciled across his back," one police officer remarked.

Stolen prison property and the fashion *faux-pas* aside, the music lover also admitted under further questioning that he was "slightly AWOL," and was supposed to be serving out the rest of his original term under house arrest.

The guy was returned to the slammer, and is now free to wear his bright orange outfit up to 10 hours a day.

Oh yeah, well your sister is so dumb she didn't even know I was your brother

VIENNA

NINE times out of ten, if a beautiful woman walks into a room and you make a crack about the length of her legs, the fellow you're talking to turns out to be her husband.

It's a guy thing — part of the mystery, the mystique of men.

But what happens when the guy standing next to you turns out to be your brother — and you're cracking wise about his wife?

Police said a fight at a family wedding got so nasty that while everyone else was throwing rice, one angry man defending his wife's honor was spilling the beans about his brother's role in an unsolved bank robbery.

Wedding guests said a man's crude jokes about the mini skirt worn by his brother's wife touched off a feud that ended up in a lengthy prison sentence for robbery.

At his trial, the fellow confessed to his part in the robbery, and apologized to his brother for the unseemly remarks.

Number 2, take 3 steps forward, hike up your sweater and say "This is a stickup!"

ST. PETERSBURG

MINUTES after being robbed of his wallet, cash and credit cards by two young women, a 52-year-old Floridian told police he can't remember the color of their eyes or hair, how tall they were, or what they were wearing.

"I wouldn't recognize them in a line-up," the shaky victim confessed while explaining that the duo had tricked their way into his home, claiming their car had broken down and they needed to use his phone to call a taxi.

The still-dazed retiree said that as he answered the knocking at his front door, both women hiked up their sweaters and flashed their breasts. One was wearing a sports bra, the other was starkers, he remembered, adding they might have been trying to show him that they weren't armed.

"There's no way I would know those girls' faces. All I do know is that they were both 36Cs," he told police.

And the dog ate my homework

BANGKOK

A 26-YEAR-OLD bridegroom with no cash for his wedding was sentenced to 3 years in prison after claiming he was robbed of $2,000 in cash and a gold necklace he was planning to offer as the dowry.

The young man's ruse involved telling the wedding guests that he had forgotten the money and pendant at home and had to return there to retrieve them.

While returning to the wedding party, he told police, he was accosted by a mugger who knocked him on the head with a gun, tied his hands behind his back and made off with the valuables.

Questioned by police who said they were suspicious that the fellow's injuries seemed inconsistent with a serious robbery, the man confessed that he had staged the incident to cover up for his lack of funds.

The bride-to-be called the wedding off and — compared with what might have been — was free to try her hand at living happily ever after . . . on her own.

It Would Take a Woman 3 Days to Learn This

WINNIPEG

WHEN police officers showed up at the apartment door looking for the culprits responsible for the barrage of fruit and vegetables that were hurled at them from a 19th floor balcony, the Mounties were already there.

Well, two retired Mounties.

Well, okay, two retired Mounties in what one officer described as a drunken stupor.

Okay, two drunken retired Mounties pretending to be asleep.

Referring to them as "Dumb" and "Dumber," a petite physiotherapist told the court how the two — her boyfriend and his brother, it turns out — bombarded Winnipeg's finest with oranges, apples and cooking onions from the balcony of her apartment.

Police say they were investigating an unrelated complaint at the same address when the cornucopia of fruit and vegetables began raining down on them. They also stated that the two men jumped into the young lady's bed and pretended to be asleep when officers entered the apartment.

Roused from bed, police say, one of the retired Mounties even attempted to blame his girlfriend for the attack.

The judge called the men in their 50's a disgrace to every RCMP and police officer in the country, and sentenced them to two months in jail for the assault.

And ten days to teach a woman to pull this kind of stunt

TOLEDO

A 20-YEAR-OLD wanna-be holdup artist gave himself a 220-volt eye-opener when he attempted to disable the locking mechanism on a cash register by cutting through the power cable during his attempted robbery of a downtown convenience store.

Picking himself up off his ass and demanding a bag in which to carry the loot, the guy became so rattled when the young clerk asked him if he wanted either a paper bag or a plastic one, that he fled the store empty handed, leaving his knife behind.

Police say this wily bandit was arrested several hours later when, after robbing a pizza shop, he was found standing on a street corner patiently waiting for his getaway driver.

No, No. It's *"Who's"* on first, *"What's"* on second

DETROIT

DANNY Fleisher was in love, so when his sweetheart gave birth to a bouncing baby boy, he was elated.

Randy Mendoza was also in love, so when *his* girlfriend gave birth to a bouncing baby boy, he too was elated.

The problem was, both men were in love with the same woman.

For two years after the birth, the lady in question managed to alternate and orchestrate her lovers' visits to see the child so that neither man was aware of the other's existence.

The men would finally meet, however, when mom announced that she was now in love — and leaving Detroit to marry another.

Fleisher sued for custody of his son.

Mendoza sued for custody of his son.

And the two agreed to blood tests to determine which man was the real dad.

Neither is, as it turned out, so the lady split.

When "No" means "No" and "Stop" means "Stop" and "Enough" means . . . "I'm outta here"

LONDON

A WORCESTER area housewife says her 54-year-old husband's obsession with highway markers and road signs has got to stop — or else.

The hobby began about 25 years ago, she claims, when he found a "Men At Work" sign in a hedge near their home. Now his collection has grown by leaps and bounds with every outing.

"'Stop,' 'Yield,' 'Go,' 'Slow,' you name it, he's got it," says Lynn Spanton, claiming that over the past 25 years she's watched the results of her husband's hobby fill their garage, then gradually crowd its way into every room of their house.

"It's reached a *Dead End* as far as I'm concerned," she told newspaper reporters. "I've put my foot down."

"People think I'm bragging," says Lynn's husband Grant, claiming that his collection of more than 700 highway and road signs is unique. "In Bilbao, Spain, they've named a street in my honor."

"Street or no street," his wife says, "either he rents a warehouse for this stuff or it's a 'U-Turn' and I'm leaving."

High on Joni Mitchell, spurned lover attempts to tear down a house and put up a parking lot

TORONTO

ARMED with the jealous rage of a dozen jilted lovers, an angry young man ripped the front porch off a house, tore down a garage, and demolished all 4 cars in the vicinity.

Police officers say the man had obviously been brooding since he discovered that the object of his obsession was busily planning her wedding — to another man.

Neighborhood witnesses said the love-struck lad used a front-end loader to haul 2 cars out of the driveway before starting on the front of the house. Two other cars were wrecked when the garage was demolished on top of them.

Sadly, one of the cars — a flashy, new Corvette — belonged to his ex-sweetheart's new boyfriend.

The angry young man was fined for his antics and is lucky not to be making license plates.

AND SHE SAID, "HEY BABE, TAKE A WALK ON THE WILD SIDE"

TORONTO

FOLLOWING reports that a female customer forced sex on an 18-year-old night-shift employee, gas bar owners in the north end of the city claimed they were immediately inundated with calls from young men seeking work.

At one 24-hour service station, the manager said he found 11 new applications the following morning.

Down the street from where the incident occurred, another employer claimed that 3 eager lads approached him for nighttime employment within 24 hours of hearing the news.

According to investigating officers, the incident began when the woman dropped her credit card on the floor while stepping into the cash kiosk to pay her bill. As she bent down to retrieve it, she told the young man that she had a knife. She then proceeded to have her way with him.

Police said the surge of job applicants dried up the second they issued a bulletin suggesting that the "female customer" was probably a man wearing a dress.

Oh, I don't know . . . maybe do a little reading, play a little golf, you know, just enjoy myself

PITTSBURGH

PERHAPS he decided that the protocol demanded of the judiciary was interfering with his carefree lifestyle.

Maybe he decided that the state of Pennsylvania was totally lacking in the humor department.

Maybe he just plain had it . . . up to here.

Whatever it was, an Allegheny County judge has decided to retire from the bench rather than listen to the mounting list of complaints about his behavior.

Among other things, witnesses say the judge had recently become so drunk and obnoxious that he was asked to leave a restaurant.

Next he was accused of driving while under the influence.

Then it was suggested that he was pie-faced during a trial.

Once, the Justice even reported his $60,000 sports car stolen, only to discover later that he had given it to a parking lot attendant who took a shine to it.

Finally, frustrated by the 30 odd charges made against him, His Honor took to a crowded city side-walk, hauled down his trousers, bared his ass to passersby — and announced to the world, "I quit!"

The YOW! heard 'round the world, Parts I and II

VIRGINIA BEACH

CONFRONTED by a trench-coated flasher in the elevator of her apartment, a Virginia college student smartly snagged the man's penis in the zipper of his trousers, then turned on her heels and reported the incident to authorities.

Police said the young lady was to be commended for her coolness and suspected that they'd have little trouble finding the culprit who undoubtedly headed straight to a local emergency room.

***

Meanwhile in England, another man was also looking for medical help after he exposed himself to a woman walking her dog.

A 55-year-old medical secretary said she was exercising her German shepherd in a South London park when a middle-aged man suddenly stepped out from behind a tree and waved his Johnson.

Before she got a good look at the fellow, her dog Tara, leapt out at the flasher's most vulnerable regions — and chomped down.

The lady told police that as the man limped and scurried and skulked away, she could see quite clearly that he was in a considerable degree of pain.

In hindsight, looking back, and all things considered, the lady says she preferred the killer

MUNICH

WHEN one neighbor spotted another toting what she suspected was a dead body up the front stairs of the building next door, she wasted no time reporting the incident to police.

When the suspect finally opened his door, police officers became doubly suspicious given the man's nervous behavior and what they noted as "evasive answers" to their questions.

Told that he might be a suspect in a murder investigation, the by-now red-faced gentleman confessed that what his neighbor saw him carrying over his shoulder was not a corpse, but "Coquette," his spanking new silicone sex doll.

The man then pulled out 4 other inflatable "roommates" from his bedroom, explaining that he was just "getting acquainted with Coquette" when police came a-knocking.

There are a million stories in the naked city. Unfortunately, this is one of them.

Alas, poor "Coquette," we knew her well . . .

BONN

GERMAN concept artist has requested and received permission to be buried along with his sex doll.

In seeking approval from German officials who oversee such things, the gentleman bolstered his written argument by pointing out that "many things that used to be unthinkable have become accepted."

Citing terms from his will, the 54-year-old said he wanted a simple coffin, but did not want to be buried in it alone.

In the letter of permission, government officials stipulated that for environmental reasons, his companion for his journey into the hereafter must be fashioned entirely out of latex.

"Latex has an awful smell to it," the artist stated with authority, "but fortunately, I won't be in a position to notice."

Okay, make that one-million-and-one stories in the naked city.

And I'd sure appreciate it if you guys could lay in a good supply of Canadian bacon

SYRACUSE

CANADIAN holdup artist facing up to 7 years in a New York prison claimed his jail time should be reduced because his country's dollar is worth much less than its U.S. counterpart.

Robert Moisecu of Montreal was sentenced to 7 years in prison after he was nabbed with $32,530 U.S. from a Champlain, N.Y., bank. Moisecu then wrote to the judge suggesting his term be reduced to 4 years instead.

"My Canadian criminal record — at current exchange rates — is only worth 62% of an American record," he wrote.

The judge was amused — but not that amused.

Underneath the lamp post by the barracks' gate . . . good grief Gerda, is that you?

BERLIN

POLICE were called into the red light district here to break up a set-to that had broken out between Hans (not his real name) and Gerda (not her real name either).

Happily married Hans (or so we thought) was "wandering," as some men do, through an area of the city where prostitutes gather to ply their trade.

Police say it was in the wee-wee hours of the morning when the two met on a side street within blocks of a beer garden where Hans had been having a stein or two.

"What are you doing here?" asked Hans.

"What are you doing here?" asked Gerda.

According to officers called upon to sort out the ensuing shouting match, the two were husband and wife.

Do you think I'm sexy? Do you want my body?

FREDERICTON

SOME men will do anything to attract the attentions of a beautiful woman.

Take the guy who was hauled off a tour bus by fellow travelers when, apparently dumb-struck by the beauty of a buxom seatmate, he attempted to woo her by whipping off all his clothes.

Unimpressed by his technique, his heavy breathing, his manly attributes — or possibly all of the above — the lady screamed for help, and the libidinous lout was quickly subdued by her rescuers until police arrived.

What is it about 22-year-old exotic dancers that 73-year-old men find so damned interesting?

MILAN

A 73-YEAR-OLD Italian pensioner spent close to $8,000 for a full-page advertisement in one of the country's largest newspapers, declaring his love for a 22-year-old dancer he had just seen on TV.

The former civil servant said he fell head-over-heels in love the moment he saw her on *Striscia la Notizia*, one of Italy's most popular evening programs.

Digging further into his retirement savings, this obviously intelligent gentleman then sent the young lady 100 red roses on her birthday.

Obviously swept off her feet, the dancer told a newspaper reporter that she was planning one day to phone him and say "thanks."

I'll take the history of flight for $500, Alex

TORONTO

POLICE would neither confirm nor deny that a 22-year-old man was attempting to impress his teenage girlfriend by diving stark naked from a 5th floor apartment balcony into a thicket of bushes below.

The possibility that he was showing off was one theory being investigated by police. They also added that if the young man had landed on the concrete pathway surrounding the mid-town complex — instead of the hedge — he would surely have been killed.

A second theory, police explained after speaking with neighbors, is the fellow leapt from the balcony when the young lady's father came home early from work and discovered his daughter and the young man romping about the apartment nekkid as jaybirds.

Officers are now planning to interview the rather sheepish fellow in hospital where he is being treated for a fractured hip and a broken leg.

You can't hide, Sammy, so you'd better learn to run

NEW YORK

SAMMY "The Bull" Gravano severed all "family ties" when he turned state's evidence and helped put infamous crime boss John Gotti behind bars for life.

Sammy further estranged himself by helping author Peter Maas with *Underboss*, a tell-all biography of Sammy that further exposed the underworld workings of the mob.

Gravano's reward from the state, of course, was an automatic, lifetime membership in the federal Witness Protection Program — plus a brand new face, thanks to the wonders of plastic surgery.

Since the operation, "The Bull" has become pretty comfortable in his new look. In fact, so sure is he that his new mug will, 1. attract new young ladies into his life, and 2. be completely unrecognizable by the mob, the recently divorced Sammy allowed Maas to use current photos of him in the new book.

Next time, luckless car thief says he'll try for six Samoans on a Suzuki

LOS ANGELES

WINNER of the annual award for "Worst Career Move" is the 20-year-old carjacker who attempted to steal a minivan carrying the University of Miami judo team.

The team, in Los Angeles to teach courses in self-defense, was touring the Hollywood area when the would-be car thief approached demanding cash and the keys to the van.

Before the poor fellow knew what hit him, team members sprang from the van, wrestled the poor dummy to the ground, and held him for police.

Despite the heroics, however, police say there was some disagreement among the Florida crew as to how many of them were involved in defeating the lesser prepared Californian: some claimed all 6 took part, others claimed only 4, while still others said only 2 members of the team engaged in the takedown.

I got my speedo workin'

MONTENEGRO

GIVEN Robin Williams' theory that while God gave man a brain and a penis, He supplied only enough blood for the use of one at a time, people in Serbia were left to wonder which organ it was that spurred a young man's attempt to visit his lady love.

Seems the 26-year-old had but $12 in his pocket for the $20 ferry ride to see his sweetheart in Italy.

But a promise is a promise is a promise, after all, and so into the frigid waters of the Adriatic he leapt.

The poor bugger made it little more than 60 feet — of the 90 mile trip — before a harbor patrol boat plucked the half-frozen fool from the icy water.

Officers aboard the rescue vessel said the young man was suffering from hypothermia and truly in danger when they hauled him on deck.

"He told us he was on his way to see his girlfriend in Milan," the Harbormaster told a reporter from Montenegro's newspaper, *Vijesti*. "We couldn't believe anyone could be so stupid so we called her and she said yes, they were very much in love and he had promised to visit."

As people who live by the sea will tell you, "All's swell that ends swell."

Yes, yes, I know, you were waiting for a bus . . . and where exactly was this bus going to take you?

HARARE, ZIMBABWE

A 29-YEAR-OLD driver was fired for tricking innocent commuters into substituting for the 20 mental patients who had wandered away from his bus — while *he* quenched his thirst at a roadside tavern.

Newspaper's reported that the driver — knowing he was in trouble for leaving his charges unattended — picked up 20 new passengers at several local bus stops. He then delivered them to the institution where his original passengers were expected.

Police say that while unloading the unsuspecting commuters at the hospital, the driver explained to doctors and nurses that their *new* patients were very agitated, because they refused to believe that they needed help.

Hospital officials admit it took at least 48 hours before they realized the passengers the bus driver had dropped off were not the patients they had been expecting.

Hey, like if the burglar is gone, what say I pop over and we watch TV or something

DAYTONA BEACH

A 911 operator, suspended from his job at the County Sheriff's office, had no one to blame but himself when police officers caught the smooth-talking devil using his job to get dates with lonely maidens in distress.

Newspapers say the 34-year-old operator was not only soothing and reassuring on the phone, but was gathering names, telephone numbers and addresses of the single women who called 911 to report burglaries, injuries and the like.

One young lady who called the distress line to report a break-in at her apartment said the ultra-cool, velvet-voiced creep called back to ask her if all was well, if there was anything else she needed — and to ask for a date.

Those close to the investigation say his little black book was crammed with names, phone numbers and even birth dates.

Hello? Hello?

Thank God you arrived when you did, I don't think I'd have lasted another minute

GAINESVILLE, FLORIDA

AN old-fashioned car thief was nabbed in the act when he accidentally triggered the vehicle's anti-theft mechanism which, in turn, locked him inside the car until police could come to his rescue.

Police say the hapless klutz triggered the anti-theft device while struggling to "hot wire" the sporty new vehicle in a downtown parking lot.

The fellow could have escaped, an officer explained, if he had simply used the release button on the driver's side door, but obviously panicked at what was happening and was too rattled to deal with it.

When officers discovered the man during a routine patrol, they found him doing his best to hide in the back seat.

Using sign language, a sheriff's deputy showed the guy how to unlock the door, then arrested him as he stepped outside.

When it's pot, it's pot, and when it's not, well, hell, it probably doesn't matter

CALGARY

THE age-old debate about whether a glass is *half full or half empty* found its way into a Calgary courtroom when a young "farmer" argued that his 18-month sentence should be substantially reduced because the marijuana he grew would get the average user "half stoned at best."

The fellow's lawyer even provided an expert witness — a University of Calgary botanist who testified that the wattage of the lighting in the young man's hydroponics greenhouse was inadequate to produce anything in the way of viable plants.

Nice try, but no cigar, said the Alberta Court of Appeal, unanimously agreeing that good pot or bad, the man's poor green thumb would have little if any effect on the price of his stuff when it hit the street.

You put the right lobe here … you put the left lobe there … and that's what it's all about

CAIRO

EGYPTIAN police reported that a man they arrested had performed brain surgery on a half-dozen patients in a Cairo hospital despite the fact that not one member of the hospital's staff was aware that he had never been to medical school.

Reports said the man, in fact, had nothing more than a primary-school education.

Records at the hospital indicate that the 40-year-old imposter had treated upwards of 100 patients every week before it was discovered he was not a doctor.

He had also performed at least 6 operations.

Police said the fellow had forged his medical-school degrees and claimed he had studied brain surgery at universities in both Cairo and Germany.

So far, no complaints.

Abracadabra, alakazam ... be gone, get out, scoot, scram!

SYDNEY

AN Australian magician who dazzled audiences countless times over by making his wife vanish into thin air, was recently arrested after attempting to make the little lady disappear — for good.

Investigators testified that the 70-year-old illusionist became angry and depressed when he realized that both his marriage and stage career were falling apart at the same time. So, in efforts to extradite himself from the dual predicament, he rigged his prop stage-gun to shoot *real* bullets.

The women miraculously recovered, but the magician disappeared — for 6 years.

Pyromaniac, food critic, volunteer firefighter, say this is a pretty impressive resume!

MELBOURNE

A VOLUNTEER firefighter set fire to his old primary school so teachers and students would get to see him — all decked out in his uniform — coming to the rescue.

A handsome sight, several young school girls agreed.

Investigating officers, suspicious for undisclosed reasons, searched the 18-year-old's home where they found more hot goods — a collection of uneaten lunches pilfered from lockers in the school.

Testifying at trial, a school psychologist said the young Australian's poor self-esteem and his need to impress others undoubtedly triggered the lad's interest in other people's diets — as well as the arson attack.

The firefighter-foodie pleaded guilty to two counts of arson, seven counts of theft and three counts of burglary.

Why leave the toilet seat up — when it can be removed completely

BROCKVILLE, ONTARIO

A 29-YEAR-OLD Brockville man sued his dead mother claiming that before she died, she fell on him and broke *his* ankle.

He told the judge that his mother fell while getting out of a chair to dance with him.

The judge awarded the man $13,000 from his mother's estate.

Whether the settlement will encourage other young men to dance with their moms remains to be seen.

Hey, if it's not one thing, it's your mother.

The doctor made it, the patient is fine, and the bank — thank God — has its money

BOSTON

AN orthopedic surgeon had his license suspended for leaving a patient on the operating table while he dashed to a nearby bank to deposit his paycheck.

Admitting he had shown "remarkably horrible judgment," the doc blamed his quandary on a combination of tricky surgery and impossible banking hours.

First off, he told investigators, he had a number of outstanding and overdue bills to pay and desperately needed to get his check deposited before the end of the day.

Next came the spinal surgery, which, he thought, could be completed well within banking hours.

Faced on the one hand with an operation that became complicated, and the wrath of the bank and his creditors on the other, he felt he really had no choice. After a 35-minute trip to the bank, the doctor returned to the hospital and completed the operation.

Today, son, you are a . . . Santa Maria! Not again

TIJUANA

MEANWHILE, south of the border, down Mexico way, a Mexican doctor was arrested and forbidden from practicing medicine after he delivered what medical officials here have called the unkindest cut of all.

Reports said a routine circumcision turned anything but routine when a doctor's scalpel slipped during the circumcision of an adult patient and left the patient . . . well, circumcised to the quick.

Small comfort to the patient, but Mexican health officials quickly announced that the doctor was not qualified to perform the operation.

When reporters at a hastily called press conference repeatedly asked how such a blunder could be allowed to happen, they too were cut off.

Having successfully completed the "Walk of Fire," you are now qualified to "Swim With the Fries"

MIAMI

A DOZEN fast-food employees suffered first- and second-degree burns to their feet after walking barefoot over a bed of hot coals during a corporate bonding exercise.

Said a company spokesman, it is essential for people to realize that they can reach beyond their perceived limits.

More than 100 aspiring young men took part in the "firewalk."

Despite the injuries, the team of geeky, yawning management trainees deemed the gathering a huge success.

Staff at the hotel where the bonding and broiling exercise was staged said at least 1 person was taken to a nearby hospital, while the burger company provided an on-site doctor for others who had blistered their feet.

Several staffers were seen in wheelchairs the following day as they left the hotel for Miami Airport, en route to another corporate gathering at an undisclosed location.

THE LONG AND THE SHORT OF IT IS, I HAVE LEARNED MY LESSON, YOUR HONOR

MELBOURNE

CONFRONTED with the bills for mail order charges on his ex-roommate's credit card, an 18-year-old Australian pleaded guilty to a grand total of 8 fraud charges and 1 charge of credit card theft.

The embarrassed teenager, according to court witnesses, grew increasingly crimson when it became obvious that the magistrate had every intention of reading out the list of items purchased with the stolen card.

The food and hotel accommodations seemed logical enough.

So too the fact that he used the stolen credit card to pay off an overdue electricity bill.

But when it came to the pricey entry itemized as "penis enlarger," the court erupted into laughter.

Calling the whole escapade "incredibly stupid," reports show the judge handed down a "hefty" fine . . . in lieu of a more "lengthy" sentence, we presume.

Do I know what day it is? Of course I know what day it is. It's today!

TRENTON, ONTARIO

PROVING again that when it comes to remembering anniversaries, birthdays, and pretty much anything of marital significance, men know no equal — a husband once again proved this fact by forgetting his wife at a roadside service station and driving off down the highway without her.

Police say the man's wife was asleep in the car when, answering nature's call, he pulled into a service station to use the restroom.

Waking up, the lady decided to visit the ladies' room herself.

When she returned, the car had vanished.

Her husband, refreshed but obviously preoccupied with guy things on his mind, drove for close to an hour before a patrol officer caught up to inform him that his lovely wife was patiently waiting back at the service station.

He is SO going to hear about this for the rest of his life.

I'm not dialing the wrong number, *dickweed*, you're answering the wrong phone

STRATHMORE, NEW ZEALAND

A JILTED groom with enough booze in his system for a whole wedding party, pleaded guilty to harassment after dialing a wrong number 18 times and ranting at a stranger he presumed was answering his ex-fiancée's phone.

A police prosecutor told the court that the man kept dialing the same wrong digit each time he picked up the phone.

Witnesses told the court the man and his ex-fiancée had been embroiled in an earlier shouting match because neither one would shell out the money to pay for their wedding license.

In levying a fine of $200 for misuse of the telephone, the judge suggested that the fellow consider counseling for anger management and alcohol addiction — and perhaps some therapy for that dyslectic dialing digit. Otherwise he'd end up back in court.

Admitting he had been drunk and stupid, the man said he wanted to apologize to the individual he had bothered, but couldn't remember the number.

SWM with money to burn seeks new true love with sense of humor

MOUNT VERNON, N.Y.

WE'D like to think that he explained the fire trucks in the driveway and the smoke in the kitchen by telling her he was saving up to buy her something very, very special.

But the evidence somehow indicates that quick thinking doesn't come easy to this guy.

Looking for a safe place to hide $20,000 from his one and only, a 23-year-old Mount Vernon man chose the oven — a gas oven.

Firefighters say more than half of the fellow's stash was broiled, baked, burned, roasted and destroyed within minutes when the oven's automatic pilot light set fire to the stash of cold cash.

The romance too, according to neighbors, went up in smoke.

I'll have a Rorschach test and three hours of Gestalt therapy . . . to go

IZOLA, SLOVENIJA

A 45-YEAR-OLD with the weight of the world on his shoulders crashed his car through the glass doors of the local hospital, drove the entire length of the 1st-floor corridor to the nursing station — and then demanded psychiatric help.

Hospital officials told police that the fellow had shown up the previous week demanding admission but had left after an angry exchange with nurses.

(Five bucks says there's a woman involved.)

Innocent, Your Honor. I thought she was the Avon Lady

NORTH BAY, ONTARIO

A 39-YEAR-OLD man was charged with indecent exposure after a female courier was given a rude — and nude — surprise while delivering a package to his door.

Investigating officers said the man came to the door fully clothed, but when the young woman asked for his signature on the receipt-of-goods form, he went back into the house for a pen and returned wearing nothing but a pair of shoes.

The courier told police that the man then followed her as she escaped down the driveway.

The package, rumors persist, contained a new suit of clothes.

I will not talk dirty in the bedroom.
I will not talk dirty in the bedroom.
I will not talk dirty in the bedroom.

DELHI

WHEN his wife complained about his spicy language while they made love, a 32-year-old newlywed farmer — armed with several stiff drinks — stitched his lips together with a needle and thread.

Newspaper reports state that when his wife protested his filthy sex talk in the bedroom, the man poured himself several large glasses of rum, located his wife's sewing basket and set to work.

His wife said she found him huddled in a corner of the kitchen the following morning, his face badly swollen from the self-administered censorship.

The farmer, who had the stitches removed at a local hospital, claimed he sealed his lips to show his wife how much he respected her wishes.

"Pain?" he answered the doctor who asked about it, "I was too drunk to feel any pain."

Funny, I could have sworn there were 16 surveillance cameras in this joint

EDMONTON

IF there's ever an award for a 3-part documentary produced by, directed by and starring the same dumb man, it will have to go to the midnight prowler who methodically disconnected and walked off with 15 security cameras from a mid-city condominium complex.

"This is good footage, quality stuff," said a police spokesperson, explaining that the entire heist was filmed by the one camera the fellow foolishly overlooked.

Police say the fellow carried out the theft during 3 different break-ins at the site, the last one with an accomplice to help carry the loot.

"Our chances of an arrest are very, very good," said an investigating officer assigned to the case. "This guy is quite photogenic. I'd recognize him anywhere."

You'll have to speak up, Sonny. At my age I'm a little hard of hearing

TOKYO

AFTER making more than 200 "silent" phone calls to the 73-year-old girl of his dreams, a Japanese pensioner was picked up by police and confessed that he is gaga, smitten, dumbstruck, and only wants the woman's love and affection.

Police say the 69-year-old met the woman on a bus tour, fell madly in love, then began following her around when she refused his daily requests for a date.

Newspaper reports say police stepped in and arrested the love-struck gentleman after discovering that it was he who made the more than 200 silent crank calls in just over 10 days.

THIS BUD'S FOR ME

EVERETT, WASHINGTON

CHARGED with breaking into a neighborhood convenience store, a 47-year-old drifter launched into what prosecutors could only describe as a salute to the power and magic of ice-cold beer.

"I was thirsty," the fellow explained to the judge.

How thirsty was he?

Such a powerful thirst he had, so parched and dry was he, the man explained to the judge, that when he saw the cooler stocked with beer inside the locked-up store, he could all but taste the wonderful stuff.

So he smashed the window and helped himself to the frosty, tasty, golden nectar on the other side of the glass.

Surely even a judge could appreciate the nature of a thirst like that?

Well, no, actually.

While admitting that a defense of necessity is occasionally recognized by the courts as a valid reason for breaking the law, a powerful thirst was not a powerful enough reason, the judge ruled, sentencing the fellow to one year in the cooler.

Momma, don't let your daughters grow up around cowboys

EL DORADO

ADMITTING they got carried away with the spirit of the moment, two Texas cowboys pleaded guilty to shopping while drunk on horseback — in the food department of a midcity supermarket.

Calling their liquored-up ride through the store's produce section an extremely dangerous threat to shoppers, and commenting specifically on the clumps of manure dropped in several aisles, the judge levied fines of $400 against each man.

According to witnesses, the drunked-up duo rode into the grocery emporium through the front doors, and were whooping and hollering as they proceeded to make their way up one aisle and down another.

Asked what prompted such a dumb stunt, one of the downtown cowboys mumbled, "I guess we shouldn't have come uptown."

And when I get out, I'm thinking about maybe having my own show

GATESHEAD, ENGLAND

POLICE had little trouble finding Matthew Copleland when he held up a store and later robbed a man at knifepoint. During the second robbery, the 33-year-old was caught on video surveillance. During the first robbery, the cool thug gave his name and phone number to a young lady on the street in hopes for a date.

Prosecutors told the court that following the first robbery, Copeland had stopped to give his name and phone number to a young lady, suggesting she might like to join him sometime for drinks.

The video of the second robbery was shown later that same night on a televised crime show that the young woman just happened to be watching.

She called police.

And he got 9 years and an updated resume that's now reads, Dumb/Robber/Actor/Jailbird.

Lulu LaRue, all dressed in black, gave His Lordship forty whacks...

WILTSHIRE, ENGLAND

BORED with the task of monitoring students during an exam at Marlborough College, a mathematics professor fired up his laptop computer and settled in to watch a movie while the young men and women in the classroom toiled at the business of higher learning.

Things were whipping along spankingly, as they say over here, when one of the students under his glazed and watchful eye looked up from her desk, screamed, and ran from the classroom.

Seems the absent minded professor had forgotten to unplug his laptop from a giant lecture monitor behind him and had turned his attentions to a bit of porn while the students scribbled away.

Tut tut, as they say in the faculty lounge.

We don't need his name... "engineering student" pretty much sums it up

CAPE TOWN

A 21-YEAR-OLD Welsh tourist brought traffic to a standstill on a busy highway when the emergency door of the bus in which he was riding gave way, sending the young man head over heels — in this case, arse over teakettle — into the path of oncoming traffic.

Police said that the accident was caused when the fellow tried amusing his fellow travelers by baring his butt at passing motorists from the rear window of the bus.

The rear window of the bus, as the fates would have it, was also the emergency exit.

Investigating officers said the man was returning to Cape Town from a visit to a nearby vineyard and winery with a group of fellow engineering students when the half-assed attempt at mooning swung out of orbit.

A spokesperson for the hospital where the young man was treated for cuts and bruises said the young space cadet had requested that his name not be released to the press.

She could never find her car keys. She wouldn't get her lazy backside up off the couch. She wouldn't give up the remote . . .

TRUJILLO, HONDURAS

FOR 33 years she could never remember birthdays or anniversaries.

She'd spend hours hopelessly lost in the busy streets of Ampala, and couldn't bring herself to ask for directions.

She never left the bathroom without leaving the seat up.

There was something about leaving wet towels on the bathroom floor that gave her an inner thrill, and she was nuts about football and scratching her privates in public.

And then one day it happened.

Suddenly, for Juanita Maldonado the world made sense.

At the Instituto Hondureno de Seguridad Social Hospital where she had gone for her first ever physical, they discovered that she was — yes — a man!

Hospital officials explained that the doctors who had brought her into the world — and her very own parents — had failed to notice that her male sex organs had failed to develop normally and instead, had grown internally.

Today, Juan Maldonado, which is now what he is renamed, is out there in public, belching and farting and digging for lint. Just another one of the guys — not that there's anything wrong with that!